MW00934415

What To Expect From A Police Academy

Useful Tips, Suggestions, and Pearls of Wisdom To Help Prepare You For Your Own Academy

By

Shawn Kinsey

authorHOUSE™

1663 LIBERTY DRIVE, SUITE 200
BLOOMINGTON, INDIANA 47403
(800) 839-8640
WWW.AUTHORHOUSE.COM

First published by AuthorHouse 01/31/05

ISBN: 1-4208-0483-9 (e)
ISBN: 1-4208-0482-0 (sc)

Library of Congress Control Number: 2004098203

Printed in the United States of America
Bloomington, Indiana

This book is printed on acid-free paper.

Here to There

We're there during the day
We're there during the night
So don't you worry
Just grab your pillow and just sleep tight

We'll be out in the rain
We'll be out in the snow
So you feel secure at home with your family
Watching your favorite show

We took this job
To serve and protect
So please don't be mad
When we save your child from your neglect

We may not all be
That perfect bunch
But you can rest assure
We will jump right in and take that punch

We patrol your streets
Late, late at night
Leaving our family home alone
So we can go break up your fight

We do this out of love and passion
Not out of what we can get
We do it to keep you and your family safe
Yes, we even do it for your pet

So the next time you see a cop
Would it hurt you to just say hi
Instead of tilting up your head and nose
And rolling back your eyes

If it's not much to ask
Would you mind including us in a prayer?
Because it may just give us the strength we need
To get us....from here to there

Written by:
Shawn Kinsey

In Memory of

Robert and Frances McQuillan

Table of Contents

Preface

At a very young age, my dream was to become a police officer. The day I realized this, I lived my life to the fullest, keeping my mind on the career I wanted to pursue and choosing my actions wisely.

My taste of reality came to me on a chilly, March morning in Phoenix, Arizona. As I arrived for my first day of police training, I was nervous but very excited. I was taking the initial steps toward my dream career. As a young boy, my dreams of becoming a police officer were filled with images of driving cop cars, chasing the bad guys, and being the "Superman" of the world. After a few short days in the academy, my dreams became reality, and I soon realized that there was a lot that I was not prepared for.

Throughout my academy, learning came to me by trial and error. Unfortunately, it happened more from error than trial. At last, that glorious day had arrived. Shielded with my, "Golden Badge of Honor", I accomplished my goal and graduated from the police academy. As proud as I was of myself, one thought came to mind, "If I had only known."

My hope for you as future law enforcement officers is to be ahead of the game. These pearls of wisdom, useful tips, and practical advice were compiled to help you succeed in fulfilling your dream of becoming a police officer.

Here it is: The "If I had only knowns!"

Chapter One-----Reassurance of oneself:

As children, we were all asked the question, "What do you want to be when you grow up?" Law enforcement was our answer to that question everyone asked us as children. Some had dreams of becoming a singer, an actor, or even the next Michael Jordan; who knows, maybe even a teacher or a doctor. No matter which career people choose in their life, we (choosing law enforcement) have all shared the same exciting dream. Deep down inside of us, we possess the fundamental belief of good versus evil. We have the desire to go out and get the bad guys. Why is that? Well, that is because we, as human beings, know what is right and wrong, and we have to decide which side of the fence we want to be on. We chose law enforcement because we wanted to be the, "Good Guys".

You may have also chosen this career because you admired a family member in their role as a law enforcement officer or because you wanted to become the superhero you watched on television or read about in comic books. Or simply because, at one time in your life, a law enforcement officer made a positive impact in your life and now you want to return the favor. Whatever the case may be, this is the point you have reached in your life and the path you have decided to take.

What do you think the definition of law enforcement is? Well, some say it is the career that many people love and admire and that many other people love to hate. It comes with both positive and negative stereotypes. We have all heard them. We are the ones that people love to have around when their lives are in danger but hate to see when they make a mistake or break the law. No one remembers when we are right, but when we are wrong, no one forgets.

We go to places people do not like to talk about. We see things that most people do not even want to know exist, things most people would only see in a nightmare. We deal with people from all walks of life - the good, the bad and the ugly. On a daily basis, we leave our families, our homes, and our safe havens to go out on the streets and put our lives on the line. All in a days work? Not in this job. Law enforcement does not just become a career or a job; it becomes a way of life. It requires dedication, commitment and personal sacrifice. Only a select few have what it takes to work in law enforcement.

The qualities all law enforcement officers must have, include, excellent communication skills, good common sense, awareness of your surroundings, honesty and integrity. You must deal with situations that arise with courage and undaunting fear, by finding a power that only lies within. When all is said and done, you walk away, no questions asked, never looking back and return the next day to do it all over again.

Rarely will you receive a pat on the back, a heartfelt thanks, or a job well done. You do it because it is the passion that you have inside yourself; the passion to do the things you do everyday. Self-gratification comes from helping that certain person in need. This is why you are here, reading this book. It is our answer to the question, "What do you want to be when you grow up?"

Chapter Two-----Preparing yourself mentally and physically:

This chapter was written to give you some tips on how to mentally and physically prepare yourself for what you are going to experience when you strive to achieve your ultimate career goal.

You need to understand that you will, more than likely, experience several days, if not everyday, of personal stress throughout your training at the academy. Expect it, because not being surprised is ammo in itself. Don't let it frighten you. You will need to be stressed out to a certain extent to find out if you can manage everyday stress in a positive way. You also need to know that your academy will, more than likely, be similar to a Military Boot Camp. Several police academies that I know of are Para-Military, so if you have prior military experience, you won't be too surprised. If not, well now you know what you may experience.

How will you handle the stress that comes with the job? That is the question. You will have days when you will not know what to think, because you are overloaded with particular tasks or assignments. You may even have days where you will experience personal doubt. It may be because you were given several essays to write or laps to run around the track, but you need to continue to be strong. Believe in yourself and know that you are there to complete a mission and you WILL succeed. If you can build yourself to be mentally strong, you will do great.

I would suggest some type of personal routine. When you wake up in the morning, you need to focus on the daily tasks at hand and create different ways in which you will get them done. Write a list of short goals you need to accomplish each day. You may want to start with making sure your equipment is in order, your papers are written, and your lunch is packed. Your list should go all the way down to what you are going to be eating for dinner that night when you get home. The earlier you create your routine, the better off you will be.

Once this happens, you can become an asset to yourself and to your partners, because you are now strong enough to help other classmates with problems they may have. Do not become a crutch for others to rely on all of the time. It is imperative that they learn to be strong like you and develop their own personal mental habits, so they too can succeed. Becoming a crutch can happen very easily because people create doubt in themselves. They look for a constant strength outside of themselves instead of looking within for strength. You did not bring a babysitter to the academy to baby sit you, so do not become one for others. Teamwork and helping each other is very, very much encouraged, however being taken advantage of by a classmate is not.

Now, let's talk about preparing yourself physically. I assure you that you do not need to be six feet tall and weigh 250 pounds to be successful in this career, but you do need to keep yourself physically fit so you can properly protect yourself, as well as your partner and the public. You will come into contact with a wide variety of people

- tall, small, heavy and thin. It is imperative that you are able to handle yourself in any situation

Any type of fitness routine will definitely be beneficial to you. I would suggest a physical workout with weights at least three times a week. In addition, you may also want to create some type of cardio workout for yourself. Two times a week is definitely a plus, but you should consult a professional to properly guide you on how to work out and when to work out, depending on your physical capabilities.

On my days off from the academy, I would run a couple of miles per day with my carpool partner just to keep up my endurance. I did this so that when I got back to the academy after the weekend was over and we had to run, I would not be as tired as some of the other cadets.

You do not have to be the strongest person in the world to be in this career, but you should be in shape. Being in good physical shape may someday save your life at work, and it will also be beneficial to your health in the long run. You will definitely encounter stress in this career, so the healthier you are, the better off you will be.

While you are in the police academy, you will have some type of physical training, usually on a daily basis. You may start out running anywhere from one to three miles daily and eventually graduate to a lengthier distance, such as three to five miles. There may be an occasional seven mile run or higher. It all depends on your class instructor. (Sometimes referred to as a Class Sergeant)

Along with running, you may also have some time designated for working out with weights at a gym. This would be a good time for you to take advantage of getting paid to work out. Not only will you get paid for working out, you will benefit by becoming more physically fit and stronger. The great thing about weight training is that it will only benefit you, no matter if you are male or female. You cannot lose when you work out. You get stronger, healthier and it makes you look and feel great. When you are physically fit, you will encounter fewer people out on the street wanting to test you. What I mean by that is, there may be a "bad guy" thinking about trying to fight you. Well, if he sees that you are in good physical shape, he may think twice. So, grab those dumbbells and start building those muscles!

Along with running daily and hitting the weight room, you will also get the pleasure of experiencing hours of self-defense training. While going through these extremely necessary and informative classes, you will learn basic and advanced life saving skills and techniques. These classes are a crucial part of becoming a police officer. You will learn different types of arm bar holds, takedowns, and other techniques to help you if you were ever physically attacked from the front, behind, or while on the ground.

You may not have time to exercise on your days off from the academy, so you will need to take advantage of the time that you do get to participate in physical exercise, and carry that routine with you even after you leave the academy.

Some days, you will be over worked physically, to the extent that you may think that you cannot make it, but YOU can and YOU will. That is where this manual may come in handy for you. Teach yourself now to be mentally and physically prepared, and learn to stay ahead of the game. Good luck!

Chapter Three-----Support from family and friends:

There are going to be people in your life that will have the opportunity to experience your police academy also but through you. These people may include your spouse, children, parents, siblings, or even a best friend. You will find out that the people closest to you will help you through this strenuous time in your life, and you may not even realize it.

Your police academy will take up most, if not all, of your free time. This includes family time, but it is necessary for your time to be consumed by what you are trying to accomplish. You are being molded into someone that people will rely on in the most difficult times of their lives, and you may become someone's lifeline. It is imperative that you retain all the information you are taught. This means you will need to study, study, and yes, you guessed it, study.

Whatever you do, do not push the important people in your life away in an attempt to concentrate on your police academy. Concentrating on your training is definitely what you want to do, but do not ignore YOUR lifelines. Believe it or not, you will need these people to rely on a little bit throughout your academy. You may need your spouse to make dinner for your family so you can study, or you may have your best friend drop some bills off at the post office so you can get an extra hour of sleep. It is important for you to absorb your police academy, but do not let the police academy absorb you.

Keep yourself on level ground and do not get too overwhelmed. Becoming too overwhelmed could cause you to push those closest to you away because all you are focusing on in your life is your studies. You need to learn to stay balanced.

Chapter Four-----Study habits:

Another important topic some people may have a hard time with or may be intimidated by is their study habits. I cannot stress enough how important good study habits are needed to successfully complete your police academy.

Two crucial keys to success are excellent note taking and good listening skills. The information that you receive from all of the presentations given by different instructors is going to be information you will need on your tests or even out in the field. Make sure you pay attention, because it could save your life someday, as well as many other people. I used to jot down as many notes as I could possibly write down, if I thought it was going to help me in the future. It will never hurt you to have too many notes, but it could hurt you in the long run if you do not have enough notes. So, make sure you take notes; it will make you better prepared.

There are some people in this world that never have to study for a test and they still do well. For those of us who do not possess that ability, study habits were designed to help us be just as successful as those who do not need to study. You will take several tests throughout your police academy. Some may be physical tests that you have to perform, but most will be written. You need to train yourself to develop study habits early on in your academy, because if you do not study, you will not be prepared, and you will more than likely fail. If failing is not option for you, (which it shouldn't be) then you need to study.

If you fail too many tests while attending your police academy, they will kindly open the door for you and ask you to leave. This means you will no longer be attending class with your future partners, and you will have to find another route in becoming a police officer.

I assure you that it does not look good to other law enforcement agencies when they see that you have failed out of a police academy, so be sure to study. Not only are you going to obtain knowledge most people will never know, but you are also going to become a great asset to your community.

There may be people in your life that may walk up to you, call you, or even write you in an attempt to retrieve answers that they think only you can answer. People you never thought knew you existed will look up to you because of the knowledge you have gained. You will become a person who will be looked at by others as the one who is supposed to know everything and have the answer to every question. Even though you may not be able to answer every question, you will be given the important responsibility of having to know a wide variety of information. Therefore, I press the importance of creating good study habits.

If you have a test on Monday, I would suggest studying for this test during the weekend. If you do have an opportunity to study during the week, you may want to take advantage of it, but the only time you may have to study will likely be the weekend. I say this because you may have daily tasks to tend to at the end of each night, which may only leave you the weekend to study. Take at least two or three hours during your weekend and get to know the material that you are going to be tested on.

It has been my experience that when test day comes, it usually comes with more than one test on different material, so make sure you are prepared for all of the tests you will be taking. Allow yourself plenty of study time so you will know the material. There are different strategies that may be useful to you or that could help you create ways to become successful in studying. Flash cards are very useful tools. Write down the test questions on one side of the flash card and the answer to the question on the opposite side. I used to do that and it seemed to work pretty well for me.

If you are not provided the test questions prior to the test, attempt to create your own test questions with the information from the notes you have taken. I found this to be very effective for me as well. You can also write your study material down on paper. By writing down the material, it will enable you to remember the information better. Seeing the words written down on paper will more than likely stick out in your mind.

Another suggestion I have for you, which may also be suggested to you by training staff while in the academy, is forming a Study Group. This technique seemed to work the best for me, as far as helping to retain information. You could meet with your classmates on the weekend at a local library or a neutral location that is convenient enough for everyone to drive to. This should help increase your retention of the information the best.

I wouldn't suggest a very large study group because individuals tend to have useless chatter among group members. You will then see that you have just shown up to the meeting place and did nothing but waste your time. This will cause you to forget useful information. I would suggest splitting up into groups of six to eight people at the most.

We have all heard that four eyes are better than two; well, it is also true for the brain. The more "heads" you have, the more suggestions will be brought up in your study group.

Suggestions you get from your classmates could trigger insights that could help you retain important information that may help you with your tests. Your classmates may offer very useful advice, or

17

they may suggest some methods that have worked for them. By being in a study group with your classmates, you build a deeper respect for each other, making your comradery with one another stronger. This newfound respect for each other will carry into other tasks in the academy, such as the physical tasks that you will have to perform together as a team.

So, now it's the night before the test. You have already had your productive study group, and you have written down all the information that you need in a note pad or maybe even on a napkin. You might be asking yourself, "What do I do next?" Well, I would suggest taking a moment to recheck the information that you have just studied. With the knowledge you have gained, you can be confident about yourself and go to bed knowing that you have really prepared for that test in the morning.

Be positive and you will emerge victorious. The morning of the test, you might want to take one more look over the notes you have written down and convince yourself that you are ready for whatever is going to be dealt to you. So, remember to study, study, study!

Chapter Five-----Time management and organizational skills:

We are now going to talk about time management, organizational skills and making personal time for yourself and your family.

Time management, in my opinion, is very important to your success throughout your police academy and as a future law enforcement officer. There will be certain times in the academy where you will be given several tasks, and they must be completed at the same time. You will also find out that you will have several things to do and only one day to complete them. For example, you may have two essays to write when you get home from the academy, but you also have to make sure your boots are polished so you can pass inspection the next morning. Let's not forget you still need to iron your clothes, pack your lunch, and check all of your gear to make sure you have everything you need for the next days assignments at the academy.

These are just a few examples of how you can be overwhelmed with tasks and duties, but you need to learn how to manage your time and organize your tasks so you can complete them all.

You know that you have to get all your tasks accomplished, but which one should be completed first? I would suggest writing your tasks down on a note pad, listing them by priority and accomplishing each one accordingly. Do the most important one first. Next, take a look at your list to see which one of these tasks would take the most amount of time to accomplish, and then tackle that one next and so forth. You should look at every task or assignment as being important and they will all need to be completed.

If you are smart about managing your time properly, you will complete each task accordingly, and you will have one less thing to worry about. It will be easier to complete the necessary tasks if you can learn how to multi-task. You will be required to complete several different tasks at the same time during your career as a police officer; for example, talking on the radio while you are driving your patrol car around looking for crime. Another example of multi-tasking may be trying to get information from a victim while tending to their injury. So, you might want to train yourself now on how to multi-task. Have a loved one or a friend quiz you with flash cards while you are ironing your uniform, or have someone drill you on test questions while you polish your boots. Those techniques really worked for me!

Let's talk about personal time. Personal time is so important for you to have during times of stress and personal exertion, which you will acquire from certain tasks throughout the academy. You will not have a whole lot of personal time while you are attending the police academy, but I would suggest squeezing some time to take a breather from all of your stress and duties. This will keep you from getting burned out. When you make personal time for yourself, include your family, such as your kids, wife, husband, etc. This will show them that you still love them and you're not ignoring them. You are still putting your family first while trying to accomplish your career goal and that is really important.

I would suggest designating a particular day out of your week, taking at least a few hours from that day, and utilize it as "Family Day." On this day, you will be relaxed, unstressed and your family should have your undivided attention while they get to spend some time with you.

These moments of calmness and self-reflection will help you carry on and recharge yourself, helping you prepare yourself for the next set of tasks that you will have to handle. Taking a little personal time will rejuvenate you. Do some extra curricular activities, such as going to a movie, playing a game, listening to music, or whatever it is that helps you take your mind off of the academy just for a small length of time.

Taking advantage of your "personal time" or "free time" as you may call it, may cause you problems in the future, so be careful. It may become easy to allow yourself an excessive amount of free time as you go along, which takes time away from your studies. Do not slip into making your "free time" a habit. Make it a luxury.

The more free time you allow yourself, the harder it may be to stay motivated and focused on what is really at hand here, graduating your police academy. So, limit your free time, and determine how much free time to allow yourself by the amount of work or studying you need to get done. You need to remember that completing your police academy is necessary in becoming a law enforcement officer; long periods of free time are not.

When you create your schedule, plan your free time at a particular time of the day or on the weekend. By doing this, you will automatically limit yourself to a certain amount of free time in your day, keeping you on track.

Chapter Six-----Staying focused:

Staying focused, focused, focused, is something you need to remember to do while listening to instructors, studying your material, or while you are at a study group with your classmates. Staying focused is essential when it comes to you successfully completing the police academy. I can't stress enough to you that staying focused is extremely important. Everything you will learn throughout your academy will be the result of you paying attention and staying focused.

You might encounter days in the academy where you will lose sight of what your responsibilities are, and that could seal your fate in a negative way. I suggest you listen carefully to your instructors, be attentive, and do not be afraid to ask questions. Asking questions can be a critical way of retaining information, because when you see it on the test, you will remember the discussion you had about that material. But, you will not retain any information unless you pay attention and stay focused.

After you wake up in the morning, but before you go to the Academy, eat a healthy breakfast. Go to the police academy on a full stomach. The body demands sufficient amounts of vitamins and minerals to remain healthy and strong. If you know you are going to be running that morning, I would suggest eating something light, but satisfying. By eating, you will be more alert, and your ability to concentrate will be much greater. It worked that way for me.

You never know when your instructor is going to surprise you with a quiz. If you are not paying attention because of your lack of energy, you may fail that test. So, remember to stay prepared and focused at all times.

There may be other things that will help you to stay focused while in the academy. For example, someday you may find yourself day dreaming about your academy graduation and how you might look in your uniform on that day, or how you are going to handle certain situations when you get out on the road (in patrol). This constant day dreaming can be such a motivator in itself. If that is what you need to think about when you are going through a rough time, then by all means, allow that to be your biggest motivator.

Just remember your training will be rough on you. It is supposed to be. If everyone was able to handle the stress, strain, or the pressures of a police academy, there would never be a shortage of police officers that exists in some cities across the nation. Expect the academy to be hard and strenuous, but don't give up. It is all worth it in the end.

Chapter Seven-----Test preparation:

Now, we are going to talk about test preparation. I have created this chapter to make you aware of the importance of test preparation and what you might expect while in the academy.

You will take and hopefully be successful in completing several tests throughout your academy. Usually, you have to take several tests in one day, so preparing properly for your test will be necessary. The results of these tests will determine your successful completion of your police academy and whether or not you will become a police officer.

As mentioned in previous chapters, taking and preparing for tests is crucial to your success. You will be given several topics to learn and study each week, and you will have to take tests over this material throughout your academy. Learning this material will not only help you pass your tests, but it will be the information you will need in order to do your job once you are out of the academy and on the streets. Some of the material you will receive will be extremely intense and some may seem easy, but it is all necessary. Whether it's easy or difficult, you will need to learn it.

I will reiterate some of the same things I talked about in Chapter Four, study habits. It is necessary to go over it again so you can understand the importance of learning the given material and for test preparation. Make sure you give yourself enough time to learn the necessary material that may appear on your tests. Do not rush your test preparation, but take your time and learn the material well.

Do not stop studying until you are confident that you know the material you need to learn; however, make sure you do not over study. Once you feel confident with the material you have studied, move on to the next topic, and let the material sink into your head.

I suggest you study only the material that is necessary for the test you are going to take on the next test date. If you study material that is not going to be on your next test, your mind may become clouded with material you do not need to know, which may cause you problems on test day.

Don't worry. You will be allotted plenty of time to study all the material you learned throughout your academy before you take your final exam. So, don't try to remember everything you have read or learned all at one time. Make sure to plan accordingly.

Chapter Eight-----Useful advice and constructive criticism:

Throughout your police academy, you will make mistakes. The mistakes you or your colleges make during the academy will be caused by your lack of knowledge and that's alright.

For example, you may be given some real life scenarios and then be questioned about how you would handle them. Unfortunately, your answer will, more than likely, be wrong unless you were a police officer before. You may not complete the scenario as a police officer would be expected to, due to your lack of experience.

Do not be discouraged. You are expected not to succeed at these scenarios yet. You will be taught how to properly handle these situations by your instructors, so you can effectively deal with real life situations in the future. I remember being unsuccessful on some scenarios in my academy. For example, I was sent on a call (a scenario in my academy) where there as a man down, and that was all the information I was given. Well, upon my arrival, I noticed this man laying face down on the ground, not moving. I called out to this man but received no response. So, what did I do? I walked right up on the guy without any worries in my mind. I thought he was just passed out or something. Actually, it was a booby trap. As soon as I walked up to the guy, he rolled over, onto his side, pulled a gun (cap gun) from underneath him and shot me. I was completely caught off guard. I had no idea how to really handle this call, because I didn't have the knowledge back then that I have now. Thankfully, it was just a scenario, and I learned a lot from that day.

So remember, don't be discouraged if you do not know how to handle a certain scenario. If you can't ask questions, then do the best you can. But what ever the outcome may be, make sure you learn from your mistakes while it's still only a scenario.

You may not have a clue as to how to solve these problems other than thinking to yourself, "call a cop". More than likely, you will be told how to handle it correctly by your class sergeant or instructor. Let me warn you about your instructors now, before you enter the academy. When your instructors advise you on how to do something correctly, you might think they are being a little harsh. I say that because they may tell you in a tone of voice that may give you flashbacks of a movie where a soldier is in boot camp and he or she is getting yelled at from every direction by drill instructors. I call that verbal shock treatment. Trust me, if you ever experience being verbally reprimanded by your class sergeant or instructor because you or one of your classmates messed up or did something wrong, you will not forget it.

You will remember this incident and know how to handle it correctly the next time. You will remember what you endured the first time you completed this scenario. That's what I would consider positive reinforcement.

Do not get discouraged because you get yelled at by your class sergeant or your instructors. More than likely, it will happen several times because that's the type of environment you are in. It's called discipline, and it is good for you, believe it or not. You need it in order to be successful in this career.

Some class Sergeants may be a little more vocal than others, but whether it's "in your face yelling" or sitting at desk, discussing with you what you may have done wrong and how to do it better, it is "a form of communication". It is constructive criticism. I suggest that you take constructive criticism for what it is, a form of advice. These instructors have experienced what you are trying to achieve, and they know what they are talking about. Even if you think their methods are obnoxious or even a little harsh, it's necessary for you to learn what they are teaching you.

Listen to your instructor's advice and/or criticism, because it is all information that you will someday need to know or use. Don't let it discourage you if an instructor tells you to write a five hundred word essay because you did not follow directions properly on a certain task. Make that experience a positive one, not negative.

Your instructors have a job to do and that job is to prepare you for a critical career. They also have to make sure that you receive and retain all of the necessary information that is offered to you in the academy. It is crucial to your safety and the safety of others that you take seriously the training you will receive. If your instructors ride your back about certain subjects, consider it a favor because they are helping you learn.

Once again, accept all the advice and constructive criticism you get during your police academy. You may find out one day you need the information that was screamed at you in the academy, and you will be thankful that you listened. Who knows, you may even save a life with the information you thought was minute at the time.

Chapter Nine-----Choosing the right weapon:

Choosing the right weapon for yourself is imperative. Your weapon is a tool that you will be given and trained how to use properly throughout your police academy.

Some police agencies may already have a certain type of weapon chosen for you to use. If this is the case, it is important that you become very familiar with this weapon and its components. All the information you will need on the particular weapon that has been selected for you to use will be given to you by a trained professional firearms instructor who works at, or is affiliated with, your police academy.

It is extremely important that you listen closely to your instructors while training with your weapon. This training should be taken very seriously, because your weapon and training is not something you joke around with.

Some people going through the academy may never have had the opportunity to learn about gun safety or how a gun functions, let alone have had a chance to ever shoot a gun. If you are one of those individuals, it's okay. Do not be afraid of the unknown. You will learn how to shoot and maintain the weapon you are issued. You will also learn how to defend your weapon against any suspects attempting to take it.

Your weapon will become the greatest piece of equipment in your belt of tools. I say this because your weapon will become a very close friend to you. Sometimes a weapon may even act as a security blanket to some people. I would suggest that you avoid allowing that to happen to you. Allowing your weapon to become a security blanket may result in accidental discharges (shootings) because you may draw it in unnecessary situations.

Your weapon is a very important tool for you to have, but it should only be used if deadly force is necessary. You need to know and review your police department's use of force continuum/policies during those incidences.

It has been my experience that some police agencies allow their police officers to purchase their own weapon, or they may provide them a list of several different weapon options and types to choose from. If you are affiliated with such a department, I would suggest you get the list of authorized weapons that your department approved and conduct your own personal research on those weapons.

There are different sizes of handguns to choose from, depending on how big or small your hand may be. While conducting your research at different gun stores and looking for the weapon that fits you the best, ask questions if you are unsure about anything. I am sure the sales person would be more than happy to help you. Once you find the right size weapon for yourself, look for the one with best stopping power. Again, ask the salesperson at the gun store for their opinion. They might mention something to you that you did not think of.

I have found some gun stores to have a shooting range that they may be affiliated with, and you may have the opportunity to test the weapon before you buy it. This would be a good way for you to find out which weapon best suits you.

You may even want to seek the opinions of your instructors because they are a good source of information. Ask them what type of weapon they have and why they chose that particular weapon. You may even want to ask them if they would have any suggestions for you when it comes to selecting a weapon.

With which ever weapon you choose, make sure you know exactly what the weapon is capable of doing. You should always respect your weapon; it is not a toy and should never be treated as one. Make sure when you do choose your weapon, take care of it. While you are in the academy, you will be taught how to properly maintain your weapon. It is crucial that your weapon is clean and ready for duty at all times.

It would be best to seek the advice of your firearms instructor on how often you should clean your weapon. You will have a good feeling knowing that you can count on your weapon to be working properly because you have maintained it. While you are at your police academy, you will have days where you will go to your firearms range and practice shooting your weapon. These days may be called, "Range Days."

During your range days, you will more than likely experience different shooting type scenarios. For example, you may be taught how to handle an ambush or how to conduct a felony vehicle stop. Some of these scenarios may even be conducted at night, so you can learn how to use your weapon in conjunction with your flashlight.

You will also have to qualify with your weapon while at the range. This means you have to obtain a certain score by shooting at targets in order to become qualified to carry your weapon on duty. By doing so, you have hopefully proven that you are capable of using your weapon appropriately and responsibly. As a police officer, you will have to be recertified with your weapon, at the range. How often may depend on your department's policies.

Chapter Ten-----Graduating:

Well ladies and gentleman, this is the topic I just couldn't wait to talk about, GRADUATING.

By now, you have spent the last several months asking yourself if all the demanding classroom work and studying was really worth it. You may be wondering if all of those hot/sunny or cold/rainy days, being put through physical exertion, was really what you were going to have to endure while attempting to successfully complete your police academy.

You may reflect back to one of those crummy days when everything went wrong, and you still had to run eight miles, jump over that six foot block wall or even run through a treacherous obstacle course when you weren't feeling good. But, you completed that course, you jumped over that wall and you stumbled across that finish line anyway.

You did it because you had a dream of becoming a police officer and you called upon your inner strength to conquer your biggest task, completing YOUR police academy.

On graduation day, you will be the happiest person on the face of the earth. This is the day that you have been looking forward to for months. On this day, you will prepare yourself to look the sharpest you ever looked since you started your police academy. You may get to the auditorium early, before any spectators arrive and practice with your fellow classmates on how you all are going to make your entrance into the auditorium.   You will proudly walk down the middle of the isle or come in from the side isle, looking straight ahead, with utmost professionalism.

Time passes quickly, and the next thing you hear is the auditorium filling up with friends and family members you and your classmates have invited to see you walk across the stage. You and your classmates are now lining up against the wall, checking each others perfectly pressed uniforms, making sure there aren't any strings hanging from them or any imperfections on your uniforms. You are now standing at attention, awaiting the command by your sergeant to walk in sync with each other to center stage.

It takes all that you have in you to keep from running down the isle screaming, "I did it!" You can tell by the looks on your classmates' faces that they are trying to do the same thing. (try to keep from running down the isle, just a little advice)

The time has come to walk perfectly down the isle to center stage, which looks like it has every light in the building shining down upon it. You walk right down to the stage, and you do it proudly. On your way down to the stage, looking as sharp as can be, you see all of the people who were there for you during your struggles and your stressful times. You try not to look at your friends and family, but you just have to. When you see them looking at you, a sense of confirmation comes over you because they know you worked so hard for this day, and you deserve to be there.

As you look over, you see that your wife, mother, father, brother or sister is crying tears of joy because they are so proud of you and your accomplishments.

Now you are up on stage, and your department's Chief of Police or Sheriff announces your name to come up to them to receive your badge, your "Medal of Honor." They shake your hand to congratulate you for a job well done. You proudly take your badge and shake their hand, but you really want to hug them out of pure excitement.

You turn around and everyone you love and cherish in your life is right there, taking pictures of that moment when your dream came true. The moment comes when the loved one that you chose pins your brand new shiny badge on your perfectly pressed uniform to complete the whole package.

There is still one thing left to do before the ceremony is over. You have to walk back up to the stage with your classmates and take your Oath of Office, swearing to uphold the laws of the United States and the state you live in. You hold up your right hand and proudly say, "I DO."

You finally did it! Your dream came true because you worked hard for it. No one gave it to you, you earned it.

You have now graduated and you can call yourself a POLICE

OFFICER!

Congratulations to you.

Conclusion

In closing, I want all of you to know that I am living my dream job, and it is one of the greatest feelings in the world. Just to know that I am lucky enough to be in a position that, when it's time to go to work, I am excited to go. I love to help people, catch the bad guys and go to work to something different everyday, and I get to do that for a living. That is awesome!

I hope that everyone has the opportunity to experience this feeling of accomplishment in their lives, whether it is in law enforcement or working at a convenience store.

I feel that if you enjoy what you do for a living, then you will enjoy going to work no matter what you do. Not only do you help yourself in so many ways by being happy, but you also benefit those you work with, and your success rate in your career is so much greater.

By now, I hope you have read through the material with an open mind and know that I have personally created and put together this material for you. I decided to write this book in an attempt to help you, my future brothers and sisters in law enforcement, to understand what my experiences were and hope that it may answer some of the questions, concerns, or mere curiosities you might have about a police academy.

When I graduated from my police academy, I thought to myself, "Wow, I wish I had some insight about some of the daily experiences I encountered in the police academy." My intention for writing this book was to give that insight to future police officers and/or people interested in this line of work. This is not a book to help you cheat or find out secrets (if there are any) about the police academy. It's a book that contains information, suggestions, and advice to help guide you through your police academy.

I wanted to share with those of you interested in or going into a police academy, the experiences I had, being a police academy recruit myself. I hope some of your curiosities and/or questions have been answered, and I wish the best of success to all of you in your new career.

Stay safe and always be positive. Remember to enjoy what you're doing. If there is ever a doubt in your mind as to why you chose this career, look back to what inspired you to want to be a police officer, and you will find your answer there.

I wish all of you the happiest of days and may your lives be peaceful. Good luck to you in your future endeavors in your new career as a POLICE OFFICER!

God Bless,

Shawn

Heavenly Father

Dear Heavenly Father
Thank you for this day
If my flashlight should fail tonight
Please help me find my way

For I am out looking for evil
Like an animal hunting for pray
They act like it's a game
They lurk around in the dark, like their out at play

Dear Heavenly Father
We ask you to please keep us safe
As we are out in these streets
Protecting those who have in us their faith

We all know you exist
Some more than others
But when it comes down to it
We all know, you made us brothers

Dear Heavenly Father
Thank you for keeping us safe so far
Cause' we know it's not just the vest that protects
It's that spirit just beyond that furthest star

Written by:
Shawn Kinsey

States and their abbreviations

Alabama – AL	Montana – MT
Alaska – AK	Nebraska – NE
Arizona – AZ	Nevada - NV
Arkansas – AR	New Hampshire – NH
California – CA	New Jersey – NJ
Colorado – CO	New Mexico - NM
Connecticut – CT	New York – NY
Delaware – DE	North Carolina – NC
Florida – FL	North Dakota – ND
Georgia – GA	Ohio – OH
Hawaii – HI	Oklahoma – OK
Idaho – ID	Oregon – OR
Illinois – IL	Pennsylvania –PA
Indiana – IN	Rhode Island – RI
Iowa – IA	South Carolina – SC
Kansas – KS	South Dakota – SD
Kentucky – KY	Tennessee – TN
Louisiana – LA	Texas – TX
Maine – ME	Utah – UT
Maryland – MD	Vermont – VT
Massachusetts –MA	Virginia – VA
Michigan – MI	Washington – WA
Minnesota – MN	West Virginia – WV
Mississippi – MS	Wisconsin – WI
Missouri – MO	Wyoming - WY

Common words used in Law Enforcement:

A	Amphetamine
Abandoned	Amphibious
Abandonment	Anatomical
Abetting	Anonymous
Abortion	Apartment
Abuse	Appeal
Access	Appearance
Accident	Applicability
Accomplice	Appointment
Account	Argument
Acquittal	Arraignment
Action	Arrest
Adjudication	Arson
Administration	Assault
Admission	Assignment
Adult	Assisted
Adultery	Association
Advertising	Attorney
Affidavit	Automobile
Affirmation	
Aggravated	**B**
Aggressive	Bail
Agricultural	Bankruptcy
Agriculture	Barbiturates
Aiding	Bicycle
Aids	Bigamy
Aircraft	Bomb
Alcohol	Bond
Alcoholic	Breath
Alcoholism	Bribery
Alternate	Bridge
Alternative	Building
Ambulance	Burden

Burglary
Business

C

Campaign
Capital
Carrying
Certificate
Character
Chauffeur
Child
Chronic
Cigarette
Citation
Cities
City
Citizen
Civil
Classification
Clergy
Cocaine
Coercion
Collision
Commercial
Commitment
Competent
Competency
Competition
Complaint
Concealed
Confession
Congress
Conspiracy
Constitution
Construction
Contamination
Contempt

Continuance
Contraband
Contributing
Corporation
Correction
Correctional
Corruption
Counterfeit
County
Court
Crime
Criminal
Cruelty
Culpability
Custodial

D

Dangerous
Dead
Death
Deceit
Declaration
Defense
Disease
Disorderly
Disruptive
District
Diversion
Domain
Domestic
Drinking
Driving
Drug
Duress

E

Eavesdropping

Ecstasy	Forgery
Education	Fraud
Eluding	Fraudulent
Emergency	Funeral
Eminent	
Emission	**G**
Engine	Gambling
Enterprise	Garnishment
Entrapment	Gasoline
Environmental	Governor
Equine	Grenade
Equipment	Guardian
Escape	Guilty
Evasion	
Evidence	**H**
Excavation	Habeas Corpus
Exemption	Habitual
Explosive	Handicapped
Extinguisher	Harassment
Extortion	Hazardous
Extradition	Hearsay
	Height
F	Hepatitis
Facilitation	Highway
Family	Hindering
Federal	History
Felony	Hoax
Felonious	Homicide
Finance	Hospital
Financial	Huffing
Fingerprint	Husband
Firearm	
Fireworks	**I**
Flotation	Identification
Following	Identity
Forfeit	Ignition
Forfeiture	Illegal

Illegally	Kidnapping
Immunity	Knife
Immunization	
Impersonation	**L**
Implied	Landlord
Impound	Larceny
Imprisonment	Legislature
Incapacitated	Liability
Incest	License
Incompetent	Liens
Indecent	Liquor
Indictment	Loitering
Industrial	Luxury
Information	
Initial	**M**
Injunctions	Magistrate
Insanity	Malicious
Inspection	Mandatory
Insurance	Manslaughter
Interception	Manufacture
Interfere	Marijuana
Intoxication	Medicine
Investigation	Mentally
	Methamphetamine
J	Military
Jail	Misdemeanor
Judgment	Mistrial
Judicial	Molestation
Jurisdiction	Molotov
Jurors	Morphine
Jury	Motorcycle
Justice	Municipal
Justification	Murder
Juvenile	
	N
K	Narcotic
Kevlar	Negligence

Neighborhood
Nitrous
Nuisance
Nunchaku

O
Objection
Obscenity
Obstructing
Obstruction
Odometers
Offense
Ordinance
Organized
Oxygen

P
Paramedics
Paraphernalia
Parent
Peddler
Pedestrian
Penalty
Perjury
Pharmacy
Photographs
Plea
Poison
Police
Pollution
Pornography
Pregnancy
Prejudicial
Preliminary
Prescription
Presence
Presumptive

Pretrial
Prisoner
Probable
Probation
Prosecution
Prostitution
Psychiatric
Psychologist

Q
Quarantine
Quarter

R
Racketeer
Railroad
Rape
Reasonable
Reckless
Recovery
Recreational
Registration
Relevance
Religion
Research
Residential
Restaurant
Restitution

S
School
Scientific
Search
Security
Seized
Sentencing
Sexual

Sheriff	Tuberculosis
Shotgun	
Signal	**U**
Silencer	United
Simulation	Universal
Slaughter	University
Sodomy	Unlawful
Solicitation	Utility
Spouse	
Stalking	**V**
Statute	Vaccination
Steroids	Vandalize
Stimulant	Vandalizing
Suicide	Verdicts
Summons	Vessel
Superior	Vicious
Surveillance	Victim
Suspension	View
T	**W**
Tailgate	Waiver
Tampering	Warranty
Tattoo	Weapon
Telephone	Weight
Termination	Wildlife
Terrorism	Windshield
Theft	Witness
Threaten	Witnesses
Threatening	Wound
Tobacco	Writs
Traffic	
Transportation	
Trauma	
Treason	
Trespass	
Trial	
Truancy	

I would like to thank the following people who have given me inspiration and direction while creating this book for you.

Jackie and Dan Reed, Nicole Goellner, Lee Goellner, Lolita Lee, John T. Baker III,

John W. Baker, Sonny Kinsey, Lee Cummings, The Sanfillippo's, Denise Palmer and MCSO.

To the rest of my family and friends, an extra special thanks to you for your love and support.

About The Author

Shawn Kinsey has been a Police Officer for the past 3 ½ years. He is dedicated to making this book a success by helping future Law Enforcement Officers through the grueling and exciting aspects of a Police Academy, making them a success as well.

Shawn will bring them closer to their dreams of completing the Academy and becoming a Law Enforcement Officer.

Printed in the United States
25833LVS00003B/529-558

9 781420 804829